I0483097

Social Media Unplugged

Social Media Unleashed, Gain new customers, & utilize all Social Media Platforms

By
Robert Nichols

Table of Contents

Dedication

I would like to dedicate this book to my parents for their guidance and support along the way.

My lovely wife, thanks for your endless support over the years. Love Ya!

This is also a great time to put my daughter's name in the book. She can say her name is in Daddy's book. Love Ya Nadra!!

Foreword

I am a Social Media & Mobile Applications trainer with broad experience in all aspects of online marketing. I am specialized in the effective use of online, mobile, SEO and social media marketing platforms. I work closely with SME and professionals to optimize these platforms in order to grow their business. My training and consultation has helped many businesses on LinkedIn, Facebook, Twitter and YouTube to name a few, pushed new boundaries in the competitive world of online marketing and advertising...

"Robert is fun to work with. We have been able to achieve many milestones with his remarkable strategies in social media marketing. I have no doubt of their capability and strongly recommend anyone to engage his services"...Lina Roseli, Creative Director-Lara Nichols Agency

"He has the unique ability to drill down into a product or service and develop a marketing plan that will drastically enhance its value proposition. This is not something he has to work hard at"...

"Robert is able to establish an online presence and marketing strategy for different niche services"...

Over the years of social media development and training, I have successfully helped businesses and organizations best use social media in procuring and developing their business relationships, engaging with their audience and improving online word of mouth communications through
effective social media marketing strategies and customized content creation. These lead to a loyal customer base for them.

Income Disclaimer

This document contains business strategies, marketing methods and other business advice that, regardless of my own results and experience, may not produce the same results (or any results) for you. I make absolutely no guarantee, expressed or implied that by following the advice below you will make any money or improve current profits as there are several factors and variables that come into play regarding any given business.

Primarily, results will depend on the nature of the product or business model, the conditions of the marketplace, the experience of the individual and situational elements that are beyond your control.

As with any business endeavor, you assume all risk related to investment and money based on your own discretion and at your own potential expense.

Liability Disclaimer

By reading this document, you assume all risks associated with using the advice given below, with a full understanding that you, solely, are responsible for anything that may occur as a result of putting this information into action in any way, and regardless of your interpretation of the advice.

You further agree that our company cannot be held responsible in any way for the success or failure of your business as a result of the information presented below. It is your responsibility to conduct your own due diligence regarding the safe and successful operation of your business if you intend to apply any of our information in any way to your business operations.

Terms of Use

You are given a non-transferable, "personal use" license to this product. You cannot distribute it or share it with other individuals.

Also, there are no resale rights or private label rights granted when purchasing this document. In other words, it's for your own personal use only.

Testimonies

"Having worked with Robert on a variety of consultations that deal with the teaching and implementation of social media, especially as a business tool, I can confidently say that his knowledge of the subject matter is vast and practical.

With many of the clients our company deals with, the methods and practicality of using social media have to be explained in a manner which is concise and satisfactorily uses the limited resources made available for marketing using this innovative medium.

Robert has helped Charles Mann clarify this type of marketing platform at numerous seminars and workshops, and has done so in an effective manner. His personal experience and practical use of social media within a business context have no doubt played a part in his expert understanding of the subject."

Abdul Awwal Mahmood, Director at Charles Mann Training & Consultancy, www.charlesmann.com.my

"I was introduced to Robert during a basketball match. After the game I shared with him what my company LJE SPORTS was about. Immediately Robert Nichols took a look at my website & my online social media and recommended that I I enhance my website. Also he implemented social media management & email marketing and now my website, social media and email marketing is up and running due to his expertise. Robert has also introduced to me other software for my company. Now I have an easy invoice plan and mail lists. I look forward to listening to Robert regarding the Mobile app for my Company!"

Bernard Williams, CEO of LJE SPORTS, www.ljesports.com

"The minute I explained my issues to Robert, he immediately engulfed himself with my issues, relentlessly working on a number of possible solutions based on my criteria. With my input and his expertise and experience he was able to develop a plan that immediately impacted my IT, and marketing capabilities. Not only was it the most cost efficient, but it was punctual, personable, and exceeded my expectations."

Anthony Nichols, Business Consultant @ Rapid Learning Institute

"Robert's Book is an intelligent, easy –to-follow guide for anyone interested in benefiting from social media. I couldn't wait to log on to my LinkedIn account to implement a number of Robert's Creative suggestions."

Joseph Morse, Inspiring Chef

"We don't know where to begin. Rob and his team really know their stuff when it comes to SEO and ranking on the search engines. We all know how important and crucial it can be to be on the first page, it could be the difference between being IN business and being OUT of business. We know that for a fact after going through several Algo changes from Google, Rob will have your website's rankings back up in no time. When it comes to anything web site related, Rob is always the guy we go to.

- Omar & Will Owners of PixPirations.com

Social Media Management for Small Businesses

Dominate Your Market, Gain new customers & utilize all Social Media Platforms

Gain New Customers by Going Mobile

In this internet age, more and more people are turning to smartphones. Why not, it's more convenient to carry around while being connected 24/7. For individuals, it's the easiest way to communicate and stay updated anytime and anywhere they are. That having said, does this also work for businesses?

Mobile phones have gone more advanced having the capabilities and functions of a PC, thus the existence of smartphones. People have been relying on  smartphones not only with their communications but also with their online transactions such as buying, selling, paying bills and even promoting their online businesses.

Here's what you may have to think about – you may either gain new clients or probably lose your existing clients. So, how does going mobile going to help your business? It works on individuals; it will work on your company as well.

Why Is Important for your Company?

Nowadays, everybody is going mobile. If you don't keep up with the trend, you will probably lose the opportunity to broaden your target market and increase your customers. It may cost you to introduce your company in a platform such as in mobile phones and tablets but it may be more financially rewarding over time.

"Mobile Statistics of 2013 – 2014
Of the world's 4 billion mobile phones in use, 1.08 billion are smartphones
91% of all adults have a smartphone."

"There was 9 million Iphones 5s & 5C's! In one weekend! In comparison iphone 4S was 5 million! IPhone 4 was approx 4 million! FACT: more iPhones were sold per second than babies were born in the December 2011!"

If prospective clients are connected 24/7, you can get ahead against your competitor by being in the front line. How do you do this? Create a website that is well-suited for mobile devices, build a mobile application compatible with all sorts of operating system and fire up an SMS promotion.

With thousands and even millions of people on mobile, your company gets an incredibly fair chance to be recognized around the world. This is an opportunity to showcase the content of your website and attract potential customers along the way. But it's not just having an application or mobile website; it should be well-thought of and possibly something interactive and responsive. You have to remember that mobile users are constantly evolving, so you have to keep up with the pace.

Mobile Websites and Why All Companies Should Have

Nearly every company has created a website for mobile because this is where they know they can easily reach their clients and potential customers. Mobile users are always on the go and if you don't reach out to your market, you may end up crumbling down. Better opportunities are within your reach so grab the chance to be at the forefront. Smart phones and internet are now two of the most widely used forms of information dissemination.

"Without having both a mobile website and mobile app, you are losing at least ¼ of your customer's share of mind!"

You may also have to understand that creating a mobile website takes important considerations in order to work well and be successful. Yes, it can be expensive to build but it will pay off sooner or later. It is probably a faster way to keep your company up and about and reach your market in the world of mobile.

To start off your mobile site:

Make your page design simple and easy to access. It doesn't have to have the frills and thrills but you want to make sure that the content is engaging enough to keep mobile users glued to your site. We are in a rapidly growing mobile market, hence you have to hold up to the constant changes and be updated on what's coming next.

Create a site that is mobile-friendly and user-friendly. These are what mobile users typically call for. In a single touch, they want to see what they really need to know since they are always on the go. They want results spot on without going through the hassles.

Gain and Retain Customers When Having a Mobile Application

Building an application compatible with mobile devices is another way of penetrating the mobile world and getting closer to your target market. Different mobile phones run different operating systems; hence it may be best to build an application that works on all available smart phone OS. This is a more advanced way to attract prospective clients and gain new customers while retaining your existing customers.

Since nearly everyone is on mobile, you stand the chance to lose your current clients if you don't keep up with the flow. Downloadable company mobile application makes your business an ever-present icon on mobile users. This makes it easy for them to access your content and see what's the latest update; perhaps discount coupons or promo offers.

Importance of Mobile Marketing

In the world where society has pretty short attention span, mobile technology has definitely earned its niche on the market. A touch of a button brings mobile users countless information in a snap. While it can be quite a breeze for companies to gain new customers, it may also be easy for them to lose prospects due to inefficient mobile application or slow and too elaborate mobile site.

Mobile internet has definitely taken over desktop internet use so it pays to have a workable mobile marketing strategy and keep it running. Otherwise, your competitor with a more viable marketing technique may take away your potential customers or existing clients.

Mobile users are rapidly growing, so take advantage of that by creating a mobile friendly site and application. However your website should be:

Informative, precise and concise specifically designed for mobile devices such as smart phones and tablets. For mobile internet users, less is definitely more.

Quick loading

Mobile users need information the fastest way it could be because they have to make decisions in a snap as they are always on the go.

Simple

Do away with unnecessary media such as Flash and images since these may retard your website. Some rich media are not compatible with some mobile phone OS.

An active participant on different social networking sites such as Facebook, Twitter, among others. Social media users now frequently use their mobile devices to access their accounts.

Internet marketing platform has drastically changed and will keep on evolving. It's the era of mobile technology where prospective customers are always on mobile now. There's nowhere else to go but join the bandwagon to keep your business alive

Ranking 1st Page Google Can Drive More Traffic

Have you ever wondered why you are not driving enough traffic to your website? Does being on the top page of Google really help you gain traffic?

Landing on the first page of top search engines can be pretty elaborate but this can be a major step to create traffic on your site. Website traffic is what most internet marketers hope to achieve in the spirit of gaining potential customers and sustaining their business. Yet, thousands are competing to be on the 1st page, so how are you going to squeeze in your company in this highly competitive fight.

"SEO – Definition: The process of affecting and improving the visibility of a website or a web page in a search engine's 'natural' or un-paid 'organic' search results"

It's a challenge but if you have the right formula, you can see your business on Google's top ranking. This means more chances your link to be clicked by thousands of users, subsequently driving traffic to your site. These are potential clients but may not necessarily become new customers. However, tremendous traffic herding your site is a positive and helpful sign for your business.

Importance of Being on 1st Page of Google

Online visibility is the key to gaining traffic and how else can your business ever be visible but to be on Google's top page. Google is a major search engine and widely used search traffic across the globe. With millions of users 24/7, it's a big opening and honor to be recognized on Google's top ranking.

So, your goal is to land on Google's first page. Why on earth do you want that elusive top ranking? I guess, for many good reasons and something that concerns about the future of your company. It may be best to talk about its importance one at a time.

More Visibility

Google usually displays the first 10 results during a keyword search and if your site's content has the right keywords, your site usually lands on the first 10 searches. You have to understand that this is very important and will be beneficial for your site. Most often than not, searchers typically click on the first ten results and may think twice on proceeding to the next page particularly if they got what they are looking for.

Greater Chances of Getting Visitors

To be on the top page means greater chances for your link to be visited by searchers. The more clicks you get the better opportunities to create generous traffic for your site. This traffic may then become your site's visitors which are potential customers and eventually may turn into new customers.

You don't want to land on the 2nd or 3rd page since many searchers usually look no further than the first page. This may provide your link a slim chance of getting visited.

Why Google for Search Engine?

Google is touted as the king of search engines. It's a word synonymous to keyword searching. It's always the first that comes to mind when someone wants to search for something over the internet. Statistics show that Google received the highest usage percentage of all search engines. This basically means that when your link is part of Google's top page result, you are more visible to millions of internet users.

Why Should Your Website Be SEO Optimized?

Through the years, search engine optimization has been proven to be one of the key factors in driving website traffic. Sadly, some have failed for obvious reasons. It may be important to note that SEO is a continuous process to be able to sustain the visibility of your site on the top search engines.

There are strategies for profitably optimizing your site but one wrong move may cause your downfall. SEO is just one of those techniques that works for a few weeks but takes a lot of time and effort to master the technique. When you are able to do that, you can enjoy online visibility which will definitely work to your website's benefit.

"Over 3 billion! Roughly 34,000 per second are performed in Google daily!"

SEO optimize your website they say. Did you dare ask why? Well, here are some valid reasons:

- To improve your site for visitors and consequently gain referrals
- To increase your website traffic
- Tremendous traffic means visitors that may convert to new customers
- To gain online visibility preferably on the first page of Google ranking
- More opportunities to boost your ranking and increase revenue
- Right choice of keywords may provide your link a steady top ranking on search results

Why ranking for your Company Keyword is Key?

Identifying the perfect keywords that prove to bring results to your company website is a crucial step in landing on the top ranking. This is perhaps as important as providing your clients product or service satisfaction. The wrong choice of keywords to optimize your online visibility may cause your company to collapse and worst, never recover at all.

"Product info and services. More than entertainment! People looking for serious stuff most of the time. Relevant information and details is the most popular area of search!"

Why worry about ranking, you ask. Ranking dictates how your link is going to perform online as far as driving traffic to your website is concerned. The first 10 results on Google search usually get to enjoy clicks from users and may never bother to look at the next page. If your site never gets to land on the top page of search engines, you may most likely fail to attract visitors to your website.

To get the top ranking, know the right keywords to use in your website's content. When searching for products or services, users normally type a keyword to get what they are looking for. You have the right keywords in your content if your link appears on the Google's first page results. This provides a better opportunity to gain website traffic.

Key Things to Remember

If you don't want to fail in your SEO campaign and you eagerly want to be on the front page of Google search.

Consider this simple technique:

1. Identify the right keywords for your content
2. Evaluate the performance of your keywords
3. Do the process again

So, it's actually an ongoing process. You don't stop finding some effective strategies to sustain your business in the online world. If you want to keep on driving traffic to your website, maintain your link's top ranking on Google search with a successful SEO strategy.

Does Your Company Do Video Marketing? Gain New Customers via Video!

Constantly evolving marketing strategies can help propel your business to new heights. The world is changing and so does your customers. To keep your business alive, go with the flow and start implementing an effective video marketing strategy.

"Viewership on YouTube

- *More than 1 billion unique users visit YouTube each month*
- *Over 6 billion hours of video are watched each month on YouTube—that's almost an hour for every person on Earth*

- *100 hours of video are uploaded to YouTube every minute*
- *80% of YouTube traffic comes from outside the US*
- *YouTube is localized in 61 countries and across 61 languages*
- *According to Nielsen, YouTube reaches more US adults ages 18-34 than any cable network*
- Millions of subscriptions happen each day. The number of people subscribing daily is up more than 3x since last year, and the number of daily subscriptions is up more than 4x since last year"

Reference: http://www.youtube.com/yt/press/statistics.html

Video usage is actually rapidly growing and it's going to be the era of video revolution. Today, video advertising is all the rage and is ever-present over the internet. It proves effective for many companies especially with the popularity of YouTube and other video sharing sites online.

Though the completion of video content may be quite challenging to pull off, you can't underestimate the power of video marketing in establishing your brand to the market. In a world of instant gratification, people will most likely watch a video than read a full length article about a product or service. But you have to tell a compelling story to earn thousands of views and get remarkable referrals.

Have you ever considered doing a video to introduce your company to the world? If not, it's not too late to start. This may help your business gain new customers while you retain your existing clients. If you need to expand your reach, then the right advertising campaign to implement is video marketing.

YouTube Stats Say You Should Have Video Content Online

With the increasing number of web video viewers every day, there's a bigger opportunity for a successful video marketing strategy. Invodo statistics show that 52% of end users who view product videos display more confidence in their purchases. That's a big number to consider when you are aiming to gain the attention of your target market.

Making your video marketing campaign to YouTube is already a great start. We all know that YouTube is one of the most popular video sharing sites today with an average of 4 billion views each day. So, that is on a day to day basis; imagine your product videos on YouTube for a week. You may not gain all their hits but you still get a percentage of viewership.

When it comes to viewership, YouTube reports that:

- YouTube visitors consist of over one billion unique viewers every month
- Videos are viewed more than 6 billion hours every month
- Video uploads happens every minute
- 80% of traffic originates from outside the United States
- YouTube is accessible on most devices
- 40% of YouTube viewers watch on their mobile devices

If you don't have a video marketing campaign on YouTube or any other video sharing sites, you may be losing a bigger chance to increase your customers and run a successful business.

Brand Your Company with YouTube Videos

Marketing your business is an overwhelming task but when it pays off, it's got to be sweet. It's not an overnight success, to begin with. But with the right marketing strategies, you may be able to see the progress over time. Video marketing has earned its niche on the web and with YouTube taking most of the viewership; it makes sense to build your brand on this popular video sharing platform.

YouTube visibility can help brand consciousness. If you are a familiar figure on YouTube videos and you happen to market your product or services, people who see you think that you are the authority. There's a certain confidence established between you and your viewers which may prompt you to start counting your hits until your videos go viral on the web.

You probably know that when a video goes viral, it means talk of the town and consequently increased views. With that happening, you must have successfully executed your video marketing strategy. You have built your brand and authority through an effective video marketing campaign. Your next step is how to convert your potential customers into new customers.

Get In Front of Millions of Potential Customers via Video

Video marketing has become a powerful tool in business. With billions of people on video sharing sites round the clock, you can get in front of prospective customers via your product videos. But they have to be engaging and quick loading since consumers easily get bored. People nowadays are always on the go and they don't have the luxury of time to wait for more than two seconds.

Consumers are always on mobile and this is the best opportune time to introduce your business via videos. Among the billions of viewers are your potential customers and you can't let that pass without doing anything. Like what was mentioned, video advertising is an extremely influential tool to gain more leads and increase your customers. According to experts (Invodo), 92% of mobile video watchers share videos with others.

So, if one prospect watch your video and share it with other 5 friends, you gain 6 potential customers. Just imagine that if it happens 24/7, you potentially have hundreds or thousands of leads. Videos are more convenient for consumers rather than reading a product content on the web.

Video's Rank Easy in Google, So Start Targeting Today

So you have your product videos on YouTube. How do you get them to be seen on YouTube and Google's top ranking? You might be thinking that it's going to be a lot of work. Yes, it may need some work but with an effective ranking strategy, your video link will definitely land on Google's front page.

Did you know that you have a bigger opportunity to be on the front page of results with your videos? With Google's "blended results," videos are more likely to land on the first 10 results pushing down the web pages. This makes video marketing more visible on the web especially on major search engines like Google.

Video marketing has already been established. All you may have to do is implement your video content the right way to be able to achieve web visibility. However, your video content must be engaging, full of information and tell a story to be able to capture your target market and win the hearts of your potential customers.

Why Facebook is a Must for Every Company?

Social media has become an essential tool for businesses in branding their company as well as in gaining new customers. It has definitely changed the business industry's environment. Companies took advantage of the worldwide popularity of Facebook and other networking sites to penetrate their target market and broaden their reach which proves to be an incredibly sensible strategy.

To date, Facebook has millions of users all over the world and still counting. With the whooping number of FB members from different parts of the world, it's so easy to establish a connection to them and introduce your brand. These users are potential customers wherever part of the world they are and if you are a multinational company and have set up your Facebook account, you have the edge to interact with your target market.

Doing business has drastically changed for the better and in a more convenient way with the proliferation of online social media. If you want your company to extend its reach and stay connected with your customers and leads, sign up your business' Facebook account.

Over 500 million Users that's Why Your Company Needs Facebook

Can you imagine connecting to millions of potential customers through Facebook? This alone is an incredible information dissemination tool that possibly creates traffic to your web page. Isn't it your goal to drive traffic on your site and gain prospects that you may be able to convert as new customers?

My company doesn't need Facebook, you say. I have more than enough customers and prospects to sustain my business. Well, in this social media age, you can find your potential clients on Facebook. Users range from ages 18 and above of varied professions and status, so you have all the reason to connect on FB. Make them feel special and you get their nod.

Facebook offers a lot of opportunities when it comes to product marketing and this is your chance take advantage of "free marketing." Many companies do their advertising campaign on this social media platform which actually works to their benefit. The use of "like", ads and fan page prove to be an effective marketing campaign wherein users who participate and give referrals get incentives or bonus.

Whether you admit it or not, you won't get in front of your million potential clients without FB considering this age and time. It's the age of social media and users are always connected round the clock. If you get your brand visible on FB, it's a big opportunity for your prospects to get to know your brand more.

Use Facebook Advertising to Target your Potential Clients

It pays to use social media advertising to be able to attract your potential clients. With Facebook's new guidelines on timeline business page, there has something to be done to keep up with your marketing plan. What's important is you follow strictly the guidelines to be able to continue with your marketing tactics.

Facebook advertising can be pretty exciting but it can be frustrating as well particularly if you don't get the right target market. However, with Facebook's settings, it allows you to target your prospects according to interests, demographic and attributes, among others. The FB page basically knows its users' age, interest and gender which provide you the opportunity to spotlight your advertisement on your target market.

FB is pretty user-friendly when it comes to your advertising plan. It allows you to target your best audience through their location, gender, age and interests. With these you are able to reduce or expand who should be viewing your advertisements. On FB ads alone your brand will be able to capture millions of potential customers which are a positive sign for your business.

Having a Facebook Fan Page is Vital to your Company

Another form of advertising is by having a Facebook fan page. This will better extend your reach to your target audience. You have to remember though that you have to separate your personal page from your business fan page to better manage your accounts.

Fan page holds a lot of opportunities for businesses that is why when you open various fan pages on FB, you will definitely find every popular brand on the market and 24/7 active. Big or small businesses, it's beneficial for them to be on Facebook because of its many features that cater to its varied users.

4 Benefits of Having a Facebook Fan Page for Your Company

Regardless of the type of your business, creating your company fan page offers your business many benefits which may include:

1. Unlimited number of fans your brand can have contrary to a personal page which is limited to about 5,000 only
2. FB fan page enjoys the benefit of indexing which may result to search engine page ranking
3. Effective advertising opportunity via FB fan page
4. Fans and other fan pages may tag your FB fan page which provide your brand the opportunity to appear on a variety of newsfeeds

Start Building your Online Community with FB

Facebook is so far the largest social media site across the globe and building your online community here may prove to be beneficial for your business. Of course, it starts by creating your FB business page then you can proceed with creating your online community. As mentioned, you can have infinite number of fans in your fan page so that should get you started.

Why Facebook, you ask.

- It is the most popular social media platform today and the largest with millions of users logging in everyday.
- It's also user-friendly with customizable advertisement platform making it easier for you to expand your online community.
- Various social media tools are compatible with Facebook

Is your brand still not on Facebook? You must be missing a lot of opportunities for your business to grow. Jump on the bandwagon and start gaining potential clients who will be able to contribute financial growth on your business. Not all may be converted to new customers but Facebook users speak volume and that is your biggest advantage since a good percentage will make the decision.

Incredible Ways to Turn Twitter Followers into Leads

A lot has been said about marketing on the internet. It's by far the best way to market your products and services if used properly. Currently, more businesses are pitching tent on social media because there is massive opportunity to explore.

There is a large host of audience on social media interacting with one another. Such kind of an audience has their own unique needs, and they must be met. Unfortunately, if you don't know how to communicate with them well, you're likely going to fail when it comes to converting them into leads that actually buy your products and services.

But you are not alone; many businesses have the right audience on social medial, especially twitter. But they don't know how to convert them into loyal customers. So they end up having them just for who they are--an audience with meaningless value. Today, you'll learn how to put a stop on that and potentially turn them into money-generating opportunities. At least there are a few ways to do that, so let's get started:

Target the people that you follow

A good business strategy highlights that that the targeted consumers are. You must target them 100% accurately if you want to convert them to leads. If you offer products for small businesses, make sure you are targeting just that--small businesses. Stop wasting your time on big industries that won't even appreciate your presence on twitter. It's about finding the right people who will care about what you want to say.

For example, you can use Twellow.com. It works pretty like yellowpages for twitter. This website gives you a list of potential customers. If you follow them, they'll likely follow you back. And when they do, they must have a purpose for doing that. No one would follow you if they don't need you or your services.

Make sure they are online at the time of your tweet more posts are slipping away without followers noticing. And that's because you are posting at inappropriate times of the day or night when majority of your audience are not online. Believe me; even if you have the greatest following on earth, posting at a time when they are not online is not the best strategy. And they won't dig into your profile to try and find out what you posted long time ago. Once they log into their tweeter accounts, they'll be looking for the latest posts, not tweets that were posted several hours ago.

Remedy

To catch them off-guard, use studies about the best times to catch your audience online. However, don't use large studies because they may not be suitable for you. Sites like SocialBro or Tweriod will show you when your audience are online. Once you create your content, schedule and post them using tools such as Hootsuite.

Listen to people

Many people complain about Twitter not generating enough business for them. Well, when you look at these people's twitter accounts, you'll notice that there's very minimal activity coming from them. They are simply not asking questions or having conversations with people. And please, quotes won't generate any business, so stop wasting your time on them.

Remedy

If they mention you on Twitter or retweet what you had written earlier, take it as an opportunity and thank them while initiating a conversation. You may ask them how their day was for example. Then you can pick it from there.

Pay attention to hashtags related to your area of expertise. Other people will ask question you can answer. That's an opportunity for you.

Have content that converts

Quotes don't convert twitter followers to leads. Creating not more than 140 characters is not a sure magnet to attract leads. Forget about those. Instead, make sure your content is pointing back to your site. Furthermore, make sure the content that you are sharing from your site is conversion-friendly. For example, it should contain newsletter signup sheet, a free download, a contact form etc.

Offer them discounts if you can

People love to receive discounts on items they buy. For example, if you follow Karmaloop's @Selkoe on twitter, you'll realize that they always have discounts for their fans. In fact, this is the best way to hook your followers without appearing spammy or overly salesy.

You can turn your twitter followers into leads in the least time possible. But you need to be smart when aiming at your audience. You don't want them to follow you when they are not giving you any value, right? Think about it.

Using Google+ to Increase Business

Google+ is one of the fastest growing social networks. Social media is already a great way to boost business and traffic, but Google+ tends to take things a step further. This is because they are already tied to Google's powerful search engine, which is one of the biggest sources of website traffic. Using Google+ alongside great SEO practices can help you grow your online brand, your credibility, and most importantly, increase your business.

Optimize Your Profile

The first step in increasing your business is to optimize your profile. Your profile is a great way to establish who you are online. You don't have to upload your entire resume; you just want to show people the face of your company. Showing people that you have a real story and have a lot to offer the world helps people see you as someone they want to do business with. You can also use your profile to subtly direct traffic to your website.

Naturally, this is also another opportunity to show up in search listings. Your profile can be optimized with SEO keywords that are relevant to the products and services that you sell. Make sure to set your profile as public to ensure that everyone can see the information you display. This will help you increase your traffic, and eventually, your sales.

Connect with People Who Want Your Product

Google+ is a great way to grow your network. Rather than relying on "friends" to promote your business, each one of your posts is searchable. This gives other users the opportunity to comment, +1, or share the information you post. You can also use the search to seek out potential clients based on keywords or phrases.

Once you connect with someone, you have the option to add them to your circles. Keeping people in your circles increases the likelihood that they will follow you in return. That means that they subscribe to every status update you post using Google+. This direct marketing serves as a constant reminder of your product or service, making people more apt to buy from you.

What separates Google+ from other social media websites is that it is a level playing field. New and established businesses have an equal opportunity to attract clients. Because most profiles are searchable, you can add influential public figures or people you are specifically targeting with your marketing campaign. This can be a great way to get an audience with people you wouldn't normally be able to connect with at all.

Promote in Communities

Google+, much like Facebook's Groups feature, has several strong communities within the network. Joining and engaging with these communities helps you to easily find people who are interested in your business. You can build a bond with them and show you care about the group simply by posting and commenting in the community.

Communities also present you with the opportunity to highlight your expertise in your field. You are in a natural, casual setting and able to recite facts or state opinions about issues in your field. This helps to establish you as an online authority figure for your field. The more authority you have, the more authentic your brand seems and the more likely people will turn to you to fulfil their needs.

Publicly Promote Your Content

One of the biggest factors in SEO is having fresh, useful content posted to your website on a regular basis. This new content will naturally bring in some traffic, but the more you can promote it the better. Unlike other social media networks, many Google+ users have no issues with clicking on links to thought-provoking articles, videos, or infographics. Because the mind-set is different and every post you make is publically searchable, you can easily use Google+ as free advertising space for your new content.

Increase Your SEO

Aside from building a business profile and engaging with potential clients, you can also use Google+ to increase your ranking in search results. Several plugins can be added to your website that display how many +1s, comments, and shares a post or page gets. This combined with the traffic you get from posting links makes your website increase in popularity, which is a common factor search engines use when displaying listings for targeted keywords. This helps you get even more traffic and further increase your sales.

Learning the Power of Pinterest for Gaining Customers

If you have embraced social media marketing for your business, then chances are you are already using Twitter, Face book and/or LinkedIn. If so, you are not alone. More than 80 percent of small business owners use Facebook to interact with their customers. Several others also use Twitter and LinkedIn. As some of the most popular social networking sites today, millions of people visit these platforms on a daily basis. And the figures keep on growing.

Apart from the aforementioned social media platforms, the image-dedicated Pinterest is now considered to be a powerful social media site for gaining customers. Once regarded as a hyped recipe site, it is currently the second fastest growing social media platform, after Google +. Although its principle of pinning and re-pinning content on boards often take time for one to get familiar with, it can be great for your online marketing campaign.

While a Twitter feed presents text, a Pinterest board consists primarily of photos or images. It can be an incredible visual demonstration of your brand. In recent times, Pinterest surpassed Twitter when it comes to referral traffic. Another study by PriceGrabber pointed out that 21 percent of Pinterest users bought something they came across on the site. This shows that if you post attention-grabbing content, Pinterest can be a fantastic marketing platform for your brand.

If used properly, Pinterest can help you gain more traffic to your site, establish loyal relationships around your business and turn followers into customers. This is the high time to take action.

Whether you are new to Pinterest or think you're a social media guru, here are proven ways to convert Pinterest users to customers.

Create a Business Account

To start with; you need to create a business account on Pinterest. But before that, it is advisable to set up a personal page to learn more about the site and find out what will work for you and what won't. Like other social media sites, learning the power of Pinterest for gaining customers requires practice. Once you are familiar with the ins and outs of the platform, you can then create a business account.

Add Credible Descriptions

A picture is worth a thousand words, and this is also true on social media. Whenever a user posts a photo, comments, repins and likes follow. On Pinterest, people will be able to notice your brand if you post quality photos. It is easy to share attractive photos on Pinterest, but it is also important to include interesting descriptions. While Pinterest offers you up to 500 characters to describe your pictures, it is advisable to use just what you require to correctly describe the relevant photo.

Merge Your Pinterest Business Account with Various Social Platforms

In order to gain more customers; you need to link your business account with various other social networking sites. Also remember to merge your photos with your own website. Once you pin an image, people should easily find it on your page. When you place your mouse above the photo, you will see a pencil-like icon on the top-right corner of your page. Click on that image and then enter your site URL on the space that shows "source." That way, users who click on the picture are directed to your site.

Interact with Your Followers and Other Users

Like any other special platform, the main purpose is to interact and know more about your followers. Thus, you need to stick to the same strategy. Follow people who follow you and also follow people who work in your business field. By so doing, you will be creating credibility among your fans. In addition, comment and repin on other photos to show other users that you are informed and passionate about them too.

Be Humorous.

Above all, have fun on Pinterest. Simply because you are in business doesn't mean you should only share photos of your company. Set up additional boards for sharing photos of your loved ones, hobbies and interests. This will give your business a personal touch other than the professional side. This will give you a competitive advantage over your competitors and allow potential customers to interact with you.

Final Thoughts

Pinterest is no longer an underdog in the world of social media. This platform is constantly growing in popularity and can be great for your company. It enables you to build relationships with your audience in ways that various other social media sites can't. Although tweets present textual content, a pin is mostly composed of pictures. Pinterest for business can offer an amazing visual demonstration of your products and company.

Tips To Maximize Using LinkedIn to Boost Business

While mainly used by job-hunters or employers looking to fill vacancies, LinkedIn can be used to boost sales and create brand awareness. The social network today reports over 259 million members scattered across more than 200 countries, providing any business an excellent opportunity to connect with its customers as well as identify new leads. But how do you use LinkedIn to build your business? While it may take some time and patience, it's not something entirely impossible .In fact, so many business owners have had their sales skyrocketing by simply tapping the power of the social media site.

Using LinkedIn to Boost Business

1. Create a separate personal & company page

Experts recommend having separate LinkedIn accounts for your company & yourself as a professional or executive. There are special "Company Pages," on LinkedIn that allow users to "follow" a particular company, and you can put up a profile that clearly outlines your company's expertise, products and services. You should make sure you complete your company's profile. In addition, use your customers as "before" & "after" stories by asking them to follow your company. On your personal LinkedIn page, you can share information or news relating to your company but you should also use it to build and maintain personal relationships with users or customers who know you personally.

2. Use appropriate keywords in heading & title

While many people assume that a LinkedIn title is the same as a heading, this is not the case. A title is important as it helps other people find you when they search on the social media site but a heading offers a great opportunity to extend the title further by emphasizing on your skills and your ideal customers. Be sure to include relevant keywords in both profile your title and heading.

3. Search for significance

What do people search for when looking for your business on LinkedIn; Is it location or industry or specialties and services? LinkedIn can provide some valuable information which you can use to know how you stand against the competition. Simply type in the keywords or keyword phrases that your customers use when searching for you in the social network's advanced search function and then try to look at what rival businesses are doing. This way, you can be able to evaluate on your current position and know what changes, if any, you need to make.

4. Ask customers for recommendations

One of the most effective ways to instil confidence and build trust is to ask your customers for recommendations. As a business owner, you shouldn't shy off from asking a few loyal customers to recommend your services or products. It's simple; if other people see many recommendations about a certain product, they're likely to develop an interest in it and potentially become buyers. However, you should make sure your request doesn't backfire by putting off some customers. Before asking them to leave a recommendation, be sure to you ask yourself if the request might be seen as annoying.

5. Try to post frequently

Another tip for maximizing LinkedIn for your business is to try to post relevant updates regularly. Google and other search engines like content that is updated frequently so posting as often as possible can help your company's pages rank higher when searched.

6. Share content

LinkedIn Today is a content aggregator of the top news shared on LinkedIn. When you subscribe to your own industry's channel news on the content aggregator, you will be able to share stories or articles you think both current customers and potential ones would be interested in. People will begin to take note of you as a good resource for useful, relevant information and they might become buyers as well.

7. Know how to welcome connections

Usually, very few people acknowledge their new connections with personal replies, yet it's something that only takes a few seconds. Always make sure you personally welcome & acknowledge any new connections. This way, you'll be able to develop new relationships and stand apart from those who are just after collecting connections.

8. Link to your Website

One unique feature of LinkedIn is the capability it provides to link your profile or your company's to up to a maximum of 3 websites or pages; you can link to your business website or personal website or else a blog. If done properly, the anchor links can also be attached to your relevant keyword phrases, further helping enhance your SEO within LinkedIn as well as on the open web.

Learn Why Having a Corporate Blog is Key to Branding your Business

Blogging has indeed found its way to the online community. It's such a big hit that it plays a crucial role in company branding. It is free and a wonderful way to advertise while directly connecting to your audience. Let it be said that a corporate blog can either make or break your business.

A business blog or better known as corporate blog has the marketing ability to capture your target market while sharing essential information about your business. This provides direct interaction with your existing customers and potential clients. A two-way exchange of ideas and opinions may be possible. A corporate blog can reach far and wide providing you the opportunity to build your business community online.

Should you start your corporate blog now or is it too late to reach out to your online prospects? It's never too late to publicize your brand over the internet. The fact is a catchy and interesting blog to introduce your business may establish brand awareness among your audience. It may not be an overnight success but a slow but sure community build up may prove to more valuable and cost-efficient.

Why Should I Start a Blog for My Business?

In this internet age, the world of brand advertising has definitely stepped up – more accessible and more highly interactive. So, why not start a blog for your business. You get the freedom to do what your audiences want and need while increasing brand awareness to your target market. This is definitely an effective way to reach out to them, encourage participation and update them of your products or services.

Blogging can be a powerful tool in marketing. Here are some reasons why.

1. It provides a two-way relation with current clients, prospective customers and business peers by replying to their comments and feedbacks

2. It allows you to talk about your brand and people behind the business opening your doors and letting your audience see what your company is all about

3. It is a cost-efficient marketing strategy where you are able to build brand awareness and promote your business as a whole

4. It promotes search engine optimization provided you have valuable content

5. It is a vital tool in acquiring higher percentage of new customers

6. It is basically your brand's voice when it comes to information dissemination

7. It is the core of all your marketing strategies in as far as content is concerned

8. It creates sales and relationship with your audience

9. It increases brand awareness thereby increasing your customers as well

Increase Brand Awareness to Expand Your Clientele

Why increase brand awareness? Brand awareness is basically letting your target market know that you exist and that you have something to offer them. With the right marketing strategy, you may be able to increase your prospects' consciousness about your business.

Corporate blogging can be an influential and valuable tool in boosting brand awareness. It allows you to engage with your target market making them more accessible wherever part of the world they are. With internet around, it is easier to connect with your audience increasing consciousness to your prospects on what your business is all about. This may incredibly help in your goal of eventually increasing the number of your clienteles.

Business blogging is one marketing plan that works. Your content speaks so much about you and your business. Well-written content speaks quality arousing audience interest. This way you are able to boost traffic on your website which means an opportunity to increase your customers. More customers mean increased sales which works to your brand's benefit.

Learn How Corporate Blogs Can Enable Higher Customer Acquisition

Content marketing, if you did not know, is a key factor in Search Engine Optimization. But your content has to be quality, interesting and attention-grabbing to stimulate your market's interest. Search engines are keen on well-written content and definitely recognize them by making them visible on search engines' top ranking. Online visibility can spark awareness on your prospects thereby driving website traffic by clicking your link on search engines.

Tremendous traffic on your website is potential customers which may eventually convert to new customers. You get to acquire higher rate of new customers while sustaining your current clienteles amplifying your company's sales and longevity. This you can achieve through your corporate blog.

One thing to keep in mind though is to publish quality content in your blog. Keep them updated every now and then holding up to your market's needs. Your audience is constantly evolving and so should your online marketing tactics. Make your content as factual and as precise as possible while capturing your prospects awareness. Brand awareness through corporate blogging increases leads and referrals who may become new customers.

Google Loves Fresh Content so Start Blogging

Blogging is a continuous process. You don't stop where you left off but instead you keep it more fascinating and fresh keeping up with your market's standard. Google, which incidentally, is a top and widely-used search engine all over the world, loves valuable content. If you want online visibility on Google, publish new content regularly and update them for everybody's benefit.

Keeping a blog is not as complicated as you would think it is. Think of it as a cost-effective way of marketing your brand to your prospects. It's also a way to connect with them and share relevant information about your products, services and company as whole. Just make sure to keep up with Google's guidelines to avoid being deindexed or removed from Google's list.

If you haven't started blogging yet or perhaps too skeptical to keep a blog site, now is the perfect time to begin learning the ropes. You do not have to be an expert on web design since there simple and easy to use blogging platforms out there like Hubspot and Wordpress. These are user-friendly platforms where you can start creating your content.

Brand awareness is a major step in promoting your business and eventually acquiring new clienteles. A more effective way to ignite prospects' consciousness is by creating a corporate blog with fresh content focusing on your business, people, philosophy and ideas.

Does it make sense to start blogging? Start now!

Why Social Media Is the Key to Surviving in the Digital World

These days, you need to engage your market before you can even hope to influence their buying decisions a little bit. That is why social media marketing has become such a critical part of any businesses' marketing campaign.

If you want to emerge victorious in this digital world, it's the right time to go social. Why now? Around two-thirds of the internet users in the US are regularly hooked to social networking sites. Companies that are active on Twitter have two times the average leads per month than those who don't use the site. Moreover, marketers who use social media for at least 6 hours per week to engage their audience and share content, usually through blogging, get 54% more leads than those who ignore the importance of going social.

How to Implement Social Media to Your Business

Seeing how important and effective social media marketing is to businesses today, you may be interested as to how exactly you're going to use it to your benefit. These tips should help:

- Think of your strengths. Assess the best things that your business has to offer, and then determine your target market. Knowing who your customers should be can be quite tricky and it can make or break your ROI. Study your market and carve out a niche for yourself.

- Open a social media account. It could be on Facebook, Twitter, YouTube, Google+, or LinkedIn.

- Look for an effective social media manager. Aside from hiring someone to do it, it might be more effective if you also use an app to run your accounts so you can set the time when the messages will be posted. It should also help you measure the effects of your social media efforts.

- Update your audience. But first, you have to ensure that your page would be interesting or have something beneficial to offer to the customers. For instance, it could be pictures of your products or videos of your customers' testimonials on YouTube.

- Establish connections. It's easier to find friends on Google+ and Twitter. You can introduce yourself to potential friends by commenting on their Google+ post, or make a mention on Twitter.

- Engage with people. Instead of directly showing your interests in advertising on social media, reach out to potential friends and followers first. Build a relationship with them at first starting with discussing, debating, or sharing good content with them. It would be easier to become friends with people this way and easier for them to help you spread the word about your business.

- Stay updated. Monitor every response or signs of engagement that you get from, such as Facebook posts, tweets, or comments, so you can respond to them right away.

Online Reputation Can Save Your Company

Online reputation management should be every business' priority. These days, your reputation is more critical in influencing your customers' decision because everyone can put up reviews, not necessarily good ones, online and potential customers can read them. It might take you years to build your business up, but it only takes a few reviews to bring it down.

What people say online about you matter. According to Nielsen's Global Trust in Advertising study, around 70% of the consumers around the world say that they trust online reviews, even those from strangers, when they make buying decisions.

According to studies, the following figures might propel you to get started on managing your reputation online:

- 59% of the consumers put more weight on customer reviews than expert reviews
- 71% of the online shoppers read consumer reviews
- 60% of the online shoppers post their feedback online and most of them tend to give positive reviews
- 80% of the time, online shoppers research about the products instead of buying
- 92% of the potential customers consider customer reviews as very helpful

Here are some tips that you can use to save your company's reputation online:

1. Google your business name. Check what people have been saying about you online.
2. Respond to negative comments. Don't ignore them. Ask these negative reviewers how you can help fix their problem with your company.
3. Start blogging. The more blog posts you make, the more those negative reviews will be pushed down in the search engine results.
4. Try press releases. These are good sources of positive content about your company, which have the same effect as your blog posts.
5. Go social. This can be a good way to connect with satisfied customers, who you can ask to give good reviews about you.
6. Join relevant forums. There are industry forums where you can establish your presence and gain more exposure for your company. Use your business link as your signature. Address the comments that are geared toward your business.
7. Start with SEO. This can help you optimize your website and build a strong and positive reputation for your company.
8. Think and rethink everything before posting anything online. Once your posts or comments are posted online, it would be harder to take them down.

Businesses, customers, employers, and employees would love to be associated with you if you have such a good reputation online. Remember, reviews about you might be these people's first impression of you, so be vigilant in looking after your reputation online.

Moving Forward in the Digital World

If you want to advance in the digital world, you need to be constantly aware of the latest innovations that will bring you closer to your audience. Those who were attuned to the developments in social media were likely among the first ones who used Facebook for marketing purposes before it became big, or used Twitter to engage their audience.

You can do the same thing too by keeping an eye on the leaders in your industry. Study their marketing strategies and try to implement or modify them, if need be, to suit your business model.

Whatever social media platform you may have to use next, the most important thing is to form a relationship with the audience before pushing your ads to their face. If they see good things about you for themselves, they would be easily transformed into your own army of promoters.

Conclusion

I hope you found the information and concepts that I have outlined in this book useful.

As you can see, improving the SEO for your company's website and creating the use of Social Media management isn't rocket science...but it does take a fair amount of work.

While utilizing Social Media and pushing your website to the first page of Google, Yahoo, and Bing is imperative, it won't do you much good if it can't be found for terms (aka keyword phrases) relevant to your business!

We specialize in helping business owners like you build a strong and meaningful presence on the web. We are also experts in optimizing both websites and Social Media Marketing and can help you get new business as a direct result.

If you'd like to see how we can help, give us a call at: +65 92730351 or visit: www.robertnichols.net

Simply complete our online form to request more information.

We look forward to connecting with you and will do our best to help you increase your web exposure, get new business and outperform your competitors!

About Author

Author, consultant, and online marketing professional, Robert Nichols specializes in helping entrepreneurs and small businesses gain a competitive advantage in their local market - both online and offline.
He helps these businesses get "found" online, en-sures that they never run out of leads, and helps them to transform these potential clients into lifetime customers (and raving fans!).

He studied and gained great experience in the US, working with multiple organisations, before

moving to Singapore. With vast expertise in the fields of Search Engine Optimisation, Web Design Philosophy, Social Media Ad Campaign Management and Keyword Research and Analysis, Robert has gained the respect of every organisation he has trained and consulted.
□

By keeping ahead of technologies and advances in digital media, Robert is a valuable asset to digital world of social media, bringing years of experience and in-depth knowledge of cutting edge industries.

A high energy, results-driven, innovative leader with demonstrated world class interactive marketing and social media skills. With extensive hands-on expertise in direct response marketing, SEO/SEM, Web 2.0, conversion optimization, online advertising, social networks. A social media professional who has a wide range of expertise when it comes to using the latest Social Media avenues such as Twitter, Face Book, You Tube and other Web 2.0 websites in order to gain online presences.

He has been involved in Social Media for the last 8 years since Social Media came to the forefront of the online world. He has been able to keep up to date with the latest technologies and methods to maximizing implementation of successful social media programs and campaigns.

Mobile Marketing Articles

Why Use Mobile Coupons in Your Business?

In business, the one thing that most people get hooked on is a discount or "freebie." Therefore, you should definitely be using these types of promotions in your business. Traditionally, coupons are printed in papers and attached to magazines and newspapers. But the traditional paper coupons are quite costly since it involves paper and printing materials.

On the other hand, mobile marketing coupons offer the same benefits as paper coupons, but with less overhead costs and expenses. In addition, coupons via SMS have a high rate of redemption compared to traditional coupons.

Most Americans own cellular phones and many of them, or perhaps most of them, always carry their mobile devices with them. Therefore, your SMS coupons are likely to be read by consumers just minutes after your send them out.

To understand mobile marketing coupons, refer to the name itself. It is one effective way of breaking the ice and penetrating to your target market by way of using their favorite gadget – the coupon. Your campaign will be easily received without having to scan on papers and wait for magazine issues. Unlike the traditional paper coupons, mobile coupons are not easy to lose and maintain dignity in redemption.

By far, redemption rates for SMS is higher than paper coupons because they are easier to claim as most people always have their mobile phones with them. This convenience alone is a contributing factor to the success rate of mobile coupon redemption.

Another thing is that, SMS text coupons are more convincing thus increasing the rate of your sales. As reports show, coupons sent via text appeals to more customers compared to the paper ones. Mobile coupons are more talked about and shared by many people. If someone gets an awesome mobile coupon offer, they are quick to forward it to their friends and family members so they can get in on the deal too. Now, you have easily added even more people to your mobile list without doing any extra work.

Using mobile marketing coupons for your business is exactly the thing that you need to capitalize on your local mobile market. It is one way to let people know that your business exists in your local community. Mobile coupons are great for branding and keeping your business in the face of your target market. Not only that, but they also help you increase profits by marketing to a list that WANTS your promotions and are happy to redeem them.

Mobile coupons are the perfect way to keep your list engaged and happy to be a part of your SMS text message marketing list.

5 Powerful Ways to use QR codes

Having a business is not easy especially if you are in a place where there a lot of competition and you have low budget for advertising. Typically, businesses do not succeed much without customers and customers will not be aware that your business exists without promotion and advertising.

In the field of business management, you will obviously hear the term "QR codes" in many strategic planning for service and product promotion. If you are new in the field, you might be wondering what is a "QR Code" and what good can it do for your business.

QR codes (Quick Response codes) are two-dimensional codes that can be read by QR barcode readers on mobile devices. QR codes appear as black modules put into a specific order in a square – like model in a white background. QR codes contain information about your business in text or URL link.

The code is initially made to decode contents and provide INSTANT information about a certain product or service. Mobile phone users can scan QR codes and immediately be directed to your website, your coupon, your online video, or to a personal message from you – and many other options.

Quickly becoming popular in Japan a few years ago, QR codes were used to track parts of automobiles during manufacturing. However, due to the possibilities of the Internet, QR codes are now used to introduce new marketing strategies that provide additional customers and higher ROI to business owners.

Listed below are five examples of how to use QR codes effectively to help your business:

1. Social Platforms

- Due to the popularity of social media, your QR codes can be attached to your web pages or social media profiles such as Facebook. That way, users can scan through the code and be directed to the information you want to get across.

2. Business Cards

- You can have QR code added to your business card to direct customers to your business website or promotional offer. If you want them to simply be directed to your website, you can set-up the QR code to do so. If you want them to simply be provided with a promotional offer, you can set-up the QR code to do that as well.

3. Packaging Products

- If your business involves sending packages to your customers, you can use QR codes to take customers to online guides and presentations about using your product. Or you can send them to a customer manual that will give them tips on using the product.

4. Press Releases

- Online press releases are one of the best ways to gain online visibility for your business. However, this visibility is intensified with inclusion of QR codes in your press releases. After being intrigued to learn more about your business after reading your press release, the viewer can simply scan your QR code with their mobile device to be taken to your website for more information.

5. Include on All Printed Advertisements

- QR codes are great for branding your business and creating awareness. You've probably noticed that more and more businesses are using QR codes on their flyers, postcards, billboards, t-shirts, coffee mugs... pretty much all of their marketing materials. The powerful idea behind this is that once the user scans the QR code, they can instantly gain access to whatever information you want them to have.

Why Your Business MUST Have a Mobile Website

No matter what business niche you are in, times are tough these days when it comes to getting ore sales and increasing profits. Businesses are forced to utilize strategies that can reach their potential and existing customers both easily and affordably.

With the amazing popularity of mobile phone devices, business cannot afford to overlook mobile marketing techniques and strategies. For instance, most mobile phone users now use their phones to surf the web. However, most businesses still do not have a "mobile-friendly" website.

Traditional websites are built to be viewed on a computer screen instead of a small mobile phone screen. So viewing a traditional website that has not been "mobilized" on a mobile phone is almost impossible. You have to scroll all over the place just to find the information you're looking for due to the limited space.

In fact, most "non-mobilized" websites don't even load at all on mobile devices. Most people use their smart phones to search for local businesses while out on the go. As soon as they hit a website that they can't navigate or use, they quickly exit the site and move on.

Can you start to see how companies are missing out on some SERIOUS business by not having mobile-friendly websites?

Here are a few other reasons your business MUST have a mobile website:

Portability and Accessibility

- Compared to a desktop or a laptop, mobile phones can be taken anywhere people go at any time of the day or night. In fact, most people keep their cell phones within reach at all times. Not only that, but people are using them more than ever to surf the web. If you want to get noticed easily and maintain the proper mobile presence, a mobile website is the perfect place to start.

Mobile Search

- Most smart phones today are equipped with applications that assist in convenient online search resources such as Google and Yahoo! Your business can easily be found when people search for products or services such as yours from their mobile devices. However, that visibility is useless if they click to get to your website and can't find the information they need because your website won't display properly on their phone.

Localization

- Mobilizing your website is the perfect way to help your local customers find you. Mobile websites have to be smaller than traditional websites, which means you have to limit the amount of content you put on them. So it's important to only put the information your visitors need while visiting your website from their mobile devices. Most people on the go are looking for your phone number, directions to your establishment, or your services list. So make sure these things are readily available and easily accessible on your mobile website.

Mobile websites can drastically increase the number of potential customers who are exposed to your business without spending a bunch of extra money on advertising.